Water

By Mike Graf

NELSON
CENGAGE Learning

Australia • Brazil • Japan • Korea • Mexico • Singapore • Spain • United Kingdom • United States

NELSON
CENGAGE Learning™

Water

Text: Mike Graf
Designer: Ivan Finnegan
Editor: Sally Cowan
Illustrations: Luke Jurevicius
Typeset in: Plantin

Acknowledgements
Photographs by: Australian Picture Library/Corbis, pp. 10, 12 top, 17, 16, 25; AUSCAPE, back cover, p. 6 bottom; Bill Thomas, p. 1; Getty Images/Stone, pp. 4, 10-11 background, 23, 26, 27 /Image Bank, p. 21 top; Reuters, p. 19; Stock Photos, front cover, pp. 6-7 background, 20, 21 bottom, 24 top and bottom; The Digital Picture Store, pp. 13; The Hutchinson Library, p. 11 top; The Picture Source/Terry Oakley, p. 18; USACE, p. 22.

PM Plus
Ruby
Where Would We Be Without Plants?
Water
Dolphins
Wildlife in the City
Desert Journal
Frogs, Fascinating and Fragile

Text © 2003 Cengage Learning Australia Pty Limited
Illustrations © 2003 Cengage Learning Australia Pty Limited

For product information and technology assistance,
in Australia call 1300 790 853;
in New Zealand call 0508 635 766

For permission to use material from this text or product, please email **aust.permissions@cengage.com**

ISBN 978 0 17 009938 7
ISBN 978 0 17 009932 5 (set)

Cengage Learning Australia
Level 7, 80 Dorcas Street
South Melbourne, Victoria Australia 3205

Cengage Learning New Zealand
Unit 4B Rosedale Office Park
331 Rosedale Road, Albany, North Shore NZ 0632

For learning solutions, visit **cengage.com.au**

Printed in China by 1010 Printing International Ltd
14 13

Contents

A Precious Resource

Water is the most abundant liquid on Earth. Water makes our planet liveable. Without water, living things could not survive.

Water is a clear liquid. It has almost no taste or smell. There is fresh water and salt water. Most of Earth's water is salt water.

The world's water has been moving between our oceans and lakes and into our **atmosphere** since the beginning of time. That means the water you drink today could be the same water that a dinosaur drank millions of years ago.

People need water to drink. We also use it for cooking, cleaning, gardening, making electricity, moving objects, brushing our teeth and washing our bodies.

Did You Know?
About two-thirds of our bodies are made up of water.

From ancient times, people have thought of ways to collect water and move it to other places where it is needed. Today, modern methods of moving water make it possible to supply big cities with enough water for millions of people. And people can now live in dry areas that have little rainfall.

Earth's population is growing, and so is the demand for water. But the amount of water on Earth stays the same. So it is important that we keep this precious resource clean and use it wisely.

Chapter 2

The Water on Earth

Water on Earth can be liquid, solid (ice) and gas (vapour). The temperatures on Earth make these three forms possible.

Two-thirds of the Earth is covered with water. Most of the water is in the world's oceans.

Smaller amounts of water are stored in lakes, rivers and seas.

Water is stored as ice on snowfields, ice caps and **glaciers**.

Some water is underground in **aquifers**. Only a tiny amount of Earth's water is found as vapour in the atmosphere.

A glacier

Windmill

Land surface

Water bore

Sedimentary rock

Layer of water trapped in sedimentary rock

Rock that water cannot pass through

Did You Know?

Water seeps into the ground and collects in aquifers. Aquifers are like giant sponges, holding huge amounts of water. The water can be pumped to the surface.

The water cycle

Water is constantly moving between the Earth and the atmosphere. This is called the water cycle.

4 Warm winds carry the water vapour higher, where it meets cooler air.

1 Drops of rain fall on land and the ocean.

3 The water vapour rises into the air.

2 The water in the ocean and on land is warmed by the sun. The water at the surface **evaporates** and becomes water vapour, which is an invisible gas.

5 The vapour attaches to smoke, dust, or salt crystals. It cools and **condenses**, and forms tiny droplets that combine with many other droplets to form a cloud.

6 When the droplets become heavy enough, they fall to Earth as drops of rain. The rain falls on land, in rivers, lakes, dams and oceans.

Did You Know?

People can't see water evaporate because single water droplets are too small. It would take about 50 billion water droplets to fill one small teacup.

Ancient Water Moving

For thousands of years, water has been used for **irrigation**. Irrigation means moving water through canals or other waterways made by people to where it is needed for crops and for drinking and bathing.

Dams are built to store water and to control flooding rivers. The first dams in the world were built for irrigation about 5,000 years ago. People used soil, wood, reeds, rocks or stones to hold back and store water.

Ruins of an ancient dam in Yemen.

The Egyptians

Ancient Egyptians used irrigation to grow crops. Egypt is in the world's largest desert, the Sahara Desert. Most of Egypt gets very little rain. In ancient times, the Nile River regularly flooded the Nile River Valley. The floodwaters left behind rich soil, which was good for growing crops.

At first, Egyptians irrigated their crops by carrying water back and forth in skin bags. Later, Egyptian farmers built dams on the Nile River. From there, they moved water along canals to their crops. Ancient farmers used shadufs to water their fields.

Did You Know?
Egyptian farmers still use shadufs today.

Today the flow of water in the Nile is controlled by the Aswan Dam.

The Romans

The ancient Romans built **aqueducts** to move water around. The aqueducts were channels carved through rock. High, arched aqueducts were built to carry water across valleys from the hills to a **distribution** centre. From there, the water flowed through lead pipes to the city. Public fountains were set up throughout Rome so people could get their own water.

Did You Know?

The aqueducts were built at an even downward slope, so that the water flowed steadily along the channels.

The Romans also built pipes to take waste water out of the city. Small drains fed into one large drain, which flowed into the Tiber River. This drain is still in use today, over 2,500 years after it was built.

The Hohokam Indians

Ancient irrigation systems were also built in North America. In the Southwest Desert of North America lies a natural water well. In 600 AD, the Hohokam Indians built irrigation ditches from the well to water their crops of squash and beans. These well-constructed waterways are still used today.

Modern Water Moving

Only about one-third of rainfall can be used by people. The rest is used by plants, soaks into the ground, or evaporates into the air.

Once the rainfall has run into rivers, streams and lakes, or collected in dams and **reservoirs** it has to get to people. Water is taken through several steps on its way to people.

Water is purified at water treatment plants. Then it is tested to be sure it is safe to pass on to people for drinking.

Modern aqueducts move vast amounts of water using large electric pumps. Sometimes, water can be moved hundreds of miles from wet areas to dry areas.

15

Living in Dry Lands

Deserts are places that get less than 25 centimetres of rain or snow a year. They are usually hot and dry. What little rain does fall, quickly evaporates. About 20 per cent of the world is desert.

Few people used to live in deserts because of the low rainfall, but now water can be brought to some deserts easily and **efficiently** through modern canals. Aquifers are found beneath some deserts. Water can be pumped from the aquifers and used by people.

The city of Las Vegas, in America, is built in a desert.
People have even built artificial lakes here.

Waste water is used to water golf courses in the desert.

The world's average rainfall compared with average rainfall in desert cities.

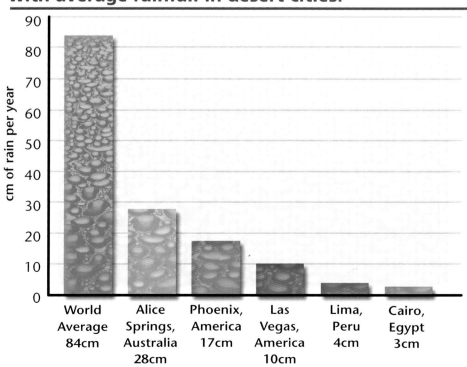

cm of rain per year	World Average 84cm
	Alice Springs, Australia 28cm
	Phoenix, America 17cm
	Las Vegas, America 10cm
	Lima, Peru 4cm
	Cairo, Egypt 3cm

Making Rain

As the world's population grows, so does the need for water. Scientists have tried to help by inventing **cloud-seeding**. Cloud-seeding can increase the amount of rain that falls from clouds.

Cloud-seeding is used in over forty countries throughout the world in areas where there are long, dry periods. Several extra centimetres of rain can be created by cloud-seeding. This might not seem like much, but when rain falls over large areas, it can make a huge difference to water storage. The extra water is stored in reservoirs and used during dry seasons or droughts.

Did You Know?
Rainfall is measured in a rain gauge.

ESTIMATED RAINFALL DURING A STORM	
Without seeding	2.50 cm
With seeding	2.88 cm

ESTIMATED RAINFALL DURING A SEASON	
Without seeding	50.00 cm
With seeding	57.50 cm

How cloud-seeding works

When a storm comes through an area, a chemical called **silver iodide** is released into the clouds from the ground or from planes.

Silver iodide forms tiny **particles**, similar to ice crystals. The water droplets in the clouds attach to the particles, then combine with other droplets and eventually become heavy enough to fall out of the cloud as rain.

Water for Electricity

Some dams are built to store water for making electricity. The dams are built in high places along rivers, and store large amounts of water. Power stations have been built below the dams.

To produce electricity, some of the water from the dam flows down pipes into a power station and through large machines called turbines. This method of making power is called **hydroelectricity**.

A turbine has spinning blades like a windmill. The force of the water makes the turbine spin, which turns a generator to create electricity. The electricity is carried through cables so it can be used in cities.

A turbine and generator in a hydroelectric power station.

Once the water passes through the turbine, it continues on down the river.

Many people like hydroelectricity because it does not make pollution like power stations that burn **fossil fuels**. But other people think that hydroelectricity is harmful to the environment.

Building dams along rivers can destroy the **habitats** of plants and animals. For example, salmon swim upstream to their original breeding ground to lay their eggs. When dams block their way, the salmon cannot lay their eggs. In some places, fish ladders have been built next to dams. The salmon swim and leap up the ladders to get back to their breeding grounds.

A fish ladder

Water for Transport

People also use water for transport. Ships and boats move people and things from one place to another. Water transportation is used on rivers, canals, lakes, seas and oceans.

Huge ships are used to carry goods over long distances across seas and oceans. Container ships carry all sorts of cargo in large containers, which are stacked on the ships' deck.

Unloading containers at a busy port.

A passenger liner

Before plane travel, people had to travel long distances on big ocean liners. Some sea journeys took several months to complete. Today, passenger liners take people on cruises. The liners are floating holiday resorts.

Barges are flat-bottomed boats that carry goods along shallow canals and rivers.

A barge

Venice

The city of Venice, in Italy, was built in a lagoon. People and goods move around the city on waterways called canals. There are 150 canals, with 400 bridges. The Grand Canal is Venice's main waterway.

The Grand Canal

Did You Know?
Many people go for holidays in Venice and enjoy getting around the city in motorboat taxis.

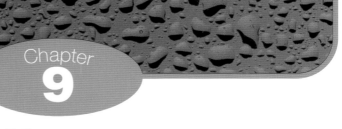

Water Pollution

Water is the most precious natural resource on our planet. But we don't always treat it well!

Different types of pollution such as **oil spills**, fertilisers, chemicals, silted water and untreated sewage are getting into our water systems. Pollution kills plants, animals and organisms that depend on water.

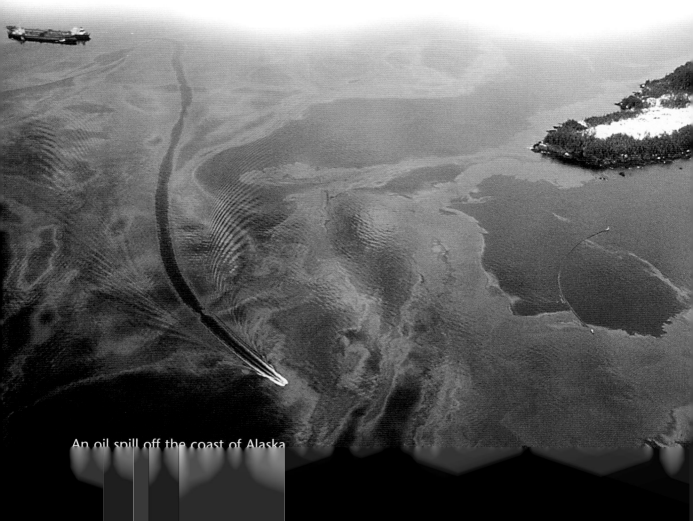

An oil spill off the coast of Alaska

Pollution also affects people. About 1.5 billion people in the world don't have safe drinking water. In some places, people get sick or die because the water they drink is polluted.

These African women have to queue for safe drinking water.

Water pollution is hard to clean up. Many governments make laws about how water should be treated and kept safe for drinking. Environmental groups try to stop water pollution from happening. They hold protests at places where they think water is not being managed properly.

Using Water Wisely

The population of the world is growing rapidly.
There are now over six billion people living on
Earth. By 2025, the world's population is expected to
be almost eight billion.

Will there be enough water for so many people?
One thing we must learn to do now is use water
more wisely.

Who uses the most water?

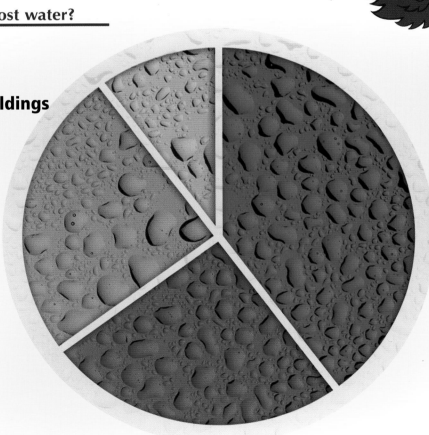

**Homes and buildings
10%**

**Industry
25%**

**Electricity
25%**

**Irrigation
40%**

Here are some things that can be done in our homes to save water:

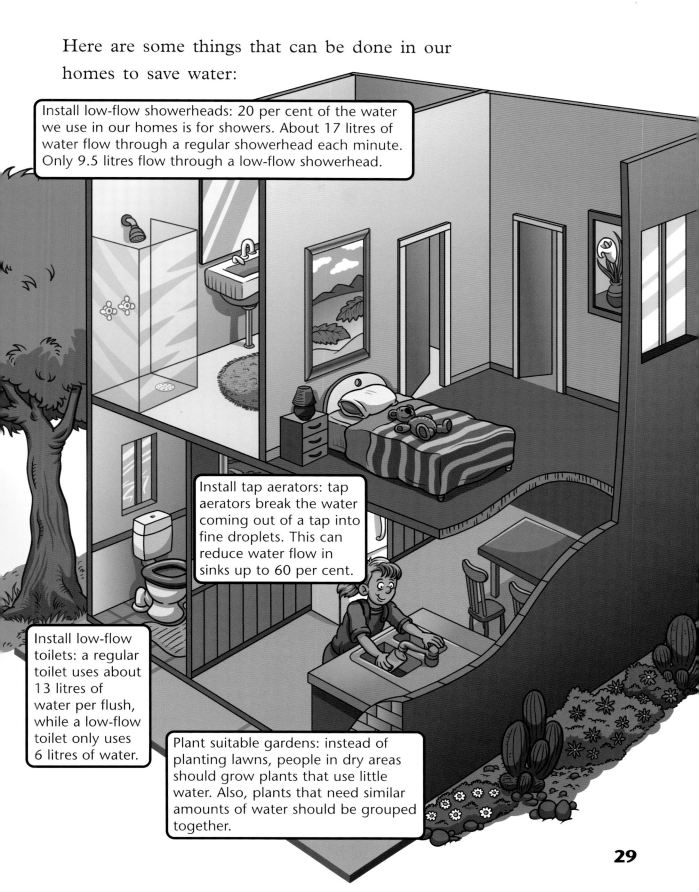

Install low-flow showerheads: 20 per cent of the water we use in our homes is for showers. About 17 litres of water flow through a regular showerhead each minute. Only 9.5 litres flow through a low-flow showerhead.

Install tap aerators: tap aerators break the water coming out of a tap into fine droplets. This can reduce water flow in sinks up to 60 per cent.

Install low-flow toilets: a regular toilet uses about 13 litres of water per flush, while a low-flow toilet only uses 6 litres of water.

Plant suitable gardens: instead of planting lawns, people in dry areas should grow plants that use little water. Also, plants that need similar amounts of water should be grouped together.

What can you do?

Here are some simple changes we can all make to conserve water.

Turn off the tap when brushing your teeth.

Water the garden in the early morning or the evening to reduce evaporation.

More ways to save water
- Take shorter showers.
- Check for leaks in sinks and toilets and have them fixed.
- Adjust the water level in the washing machine to match the size of the laundry load when washing clothes.

Sweep outdoor paved areas instead of hosing them down.

Run the dishwasher only when it is full.

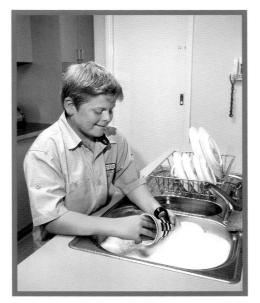

Fill the sink with water when hand-washing dishes, instead of letting the water run.

Glossary

aqueducts	pipes for carrying water
aquifers	underground pools of water
atmosphere	the layer of gases surrounding the Earth
cloud-seeding	putting chemicals in clouds to increase rain
condenses	when water changes from vapour to a liquid
conserve	to keep and use wisely
distribution	to give out or deliver things to places
efficiently	when things work well, with little or no wasted time or energy
evaporates	when water changes from a liquid to a gas
fossil fuels	coal, oil and gas
glaciers	a large, slowly-moving mass of ice and snow
habitats	places where plants and animals live naturally
hydroelectricity	electricity produced by water
irrigation	bringing water to an area through ditches or canals
oil spills	accidental leaks of oil from oil tankers
particles	very small pieces
reservoirs	areas made by people for storing water
silver iodide	chemical similar to ice crystals used in cloud-seeding
sewage	waste that is carried away in drains and sewers

Further Reading

Hooper, Meredith, *The Drop in My Drink: the Story of Water on Our Planet*, Viking, 1998

Robbins, Ken, *Water: the Elements*, Henry Holt and Company, New York, 1995